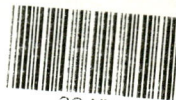
Teambuilding

Activities for young people

Vanessa Rogers

Published by

The National Youth Agency

17-23 Albion Street, Leicester LE1 6GD
Tel: 0116 285 3700.
Fax: 0116 285 3777.
E-mail: nya@nya.org.uk
Website: www.nya.org.uk

ISBN: 0 86155 298 9

© October 2003

Price: £6.50

Activities can be photocopied free of charge for non-commercial purposes.

Cover Design: Sanjay Kukadia
Editor/Designer: Katharine McKeown

Contents

ACKNOWLEDGMENTS

The Duke of Edinburgh's Award Scheme, Ann McKay (HCC Sports Development Officer), Mary Westgate (HCC Youth Service), Michael O'Connor, Jamie Scott, Mill Mead School, Simon Balle School.

Thanks also to any other youth workers, teachers or Personal Advisers not specifically mentioned who have contributed to any of the activities included.

ABOUT THE AUTHOR

Vanessa Rogers is a qualified teacher and youth worker with a Masters degree in Community Education and over ten years' experience within Hertfordshire County Council Youth Service both at practitioner and management levels. Vanessa currently manages a multi-agency youth team of youth workers, preventative workers and Connexions Personal Advisers developing creative strategies to engage with young people at risk of offending or disaffection and providing alternative educational packages.

This book is one of a mini series of five resource books developed to support youth workers, teachers, social workers, YOT teams and Connexions Personal Advisers working with young people aged between 11 to 16-years-old.

Vanessa is also the author of; **'Have You Ever ...?'** A handbook for detached workers, **'Let's Talk Relationships ...'** exploring peer, family and personal relationships with young people, **'So You Want to Work with Young People?** a training resource for volunteer workers, **'Exploring Feelings'** for work with young people under 14 at risk of exclusion or offending behaviour, **'Art Unlimited'** offering ideas to engage young people in creative projects, **'All the Right Connections'** resources for Personal Advisers, **'Work with Young Men'** a collection of activities to support and motivate young men and **'Young People and Citizenship'**.

The National Youth Agency publishes all titles, details available from its website www.nya.org.uk. Alternatively click on www.resourceplanet.com the website for Vanessa Rogers to contact the author and find out about training events.

INTRODUCTION

'How can one individual solve the problems of the world? Problems can only be solved if one is part of a team' - Nelson Mandela

This resource is packed with teambuilding ideas for young people, developing leadership skills as well as the ability to follow instructions and work cooperatively together. Hopefully it will also create plenty of opportunities to have good fun and enjoy themselves too!

Good teambuilding should create a 'whole' that is greater than the sum of its individuals whilst retaining the things that makes each person special. All team members should have an active role that plays to their strengths and develops any weaknesses. Make sure that it is clear that everybody's contribution is valued and that teamwork is not just about being good at sports. If someone is not keen to participate in group activities think of alternative roles, for example, recording or photographing the event, so that they have a clear place and purpose that balances their needs with that of the teams.

It is important to remember that although the goal set for the team may be the same, each member will see things in their own way. It is vital to recognise diversity and encourage the team to accept and use this to the advantage of everybody. This doesn't mean that everybody has to agree at all times, just that a supportive culture needs to be developed whereby members can negotiate and accommodate the views of everyone.

Before you start any session decide if you want a competitive element to the task or not. Most activities can be adapted and for all of them the process is the most important factor and the part that can be reviewed with young people afterwards.

Make sure the instructions that you give are clear and in a format appropriate for the young people you are working with, including those with special needs. If people are unclear about what is required of them they will focus on this rather than the task.

Also carefully consider the size of team that you are asking to work together. Teams larger than six can result in people either being left or opting out, resulting in stronger members of the group taking over and deciding what everyone else does! Groups smaller than three offer fewer opportunities for working together and can detract from the overall team experience.

The activities are divided into four sections:

Cooperation Games

The activities in this section encourage young people to work together to achieve a common task. To do this the group will need to talk to each other and work out ways that they can help each other to succeed. These are a good way of introducing teambuilding and can be used as a warm up or closing activity for some of the ideas in the following sections.

Trust Building Activities

The ideas in this chapter encourage and develop trust between members of the group. They build empathy and understanding that are vital to a team before attempting any of the bigger challenges.

Group Tasks

The important thing about all these activities is that they offer every member an active role without which the task cannot be completed. They recognise that everyone has different strengths and weaknesses and levels of ability.

Outdoor Ideas

These are great for good weather or for use on residentials. As most are active challenges they are not suitable for all young people, but where possible adaptations are suggested.

Cooperation Games

1. Snakes

This is a very funny game that is suitable for groups of six or more.

Aim

This game builds cooperation and highlights the need to work together.

You will need

· Nothing

How to do it

Start the 'snake' off by asking the young people to choose a partner. Explain that everyone will gradually join together until the whole group is taking part.

Each young person must lie on their stomach with their arms outstretched and hold the ankles of their partner who should lie directly in front of them.

Now ask the pairs to try and make their way across the floor. The idea is to move along as a snake without letting go of their partner's ankles!

When the young people can manage this in their pairs ask them to wriggle over and join another couple and begin to move as a foursome.

Keep this going until the whole group is joined together and moving as a big 'snake'. The more young people in the group the longer the snake and the greater cooperation needed to make it move anywhere.

2. Get Knotted!
The bigger the team the harder the task becomes!

Aim
To work together to solve a puzzle.

You will need
• Nothing

How to do it
Ask the team to form a circle, standing next to each other but not so close that they are touching.

Invite the young people to join hands with two other members of the circle, but not with anyone standing next to them. This is a lot harder than it seems! Make sure that no one is cheating and everyone is holding onto to two other people.

When everybody is in place ask the group to stop, hold the pose and look around to see what shape the team has formed.

Then set the young people the task of untying themselves and reforming the circle – without breaking hands! You should end up with the whole group back in a circle, though not necessarily all facing the same way!

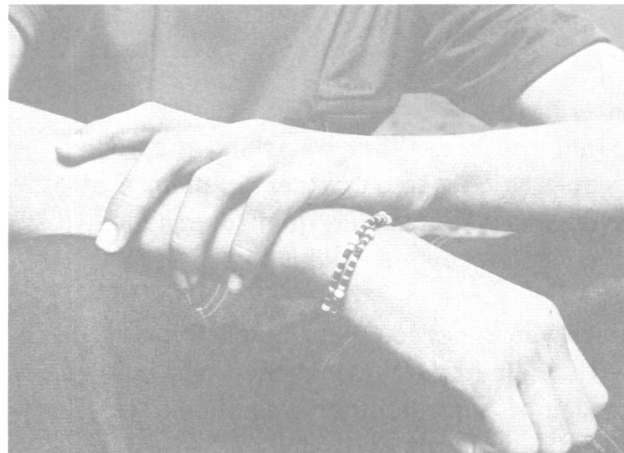

3. Paper Bridges

Divide the large group into small teams of three for this activity. Any more and there is a temptation for individuals to stand on the side and not participate, this way everyone gets involved!

Aim
To work together to design and build a newspaper bridge.

You will need
• Newspaper (broadsheets are best)
• Sticky tape
• A retractable rule
• A selection of objects (optional)
• A clock

How to do it
Hand out sheets of newspaper and a reel of sticky tape to each threesome. 20 to 30 sheets should be sufficient for a ten to 15 minute exercise; just add more if you want it to take longer.

Explain that the challenge for each group is to plan and build a paper bridge. This must include a support at each end and a horizontal span between the two. Additionally, just in case anyone tries to dodge the task, tell the young people that it must stand at least 15cm off the ground!

The winning bridge will be the construction with the longest span. If you want to make the exercise harder choose a selection of objects, such as a rubber duck, a pen, a small ball etc that has to be balanced on the bridge. No sticky tape can be used for this bit!

Using the clock, time the activity giving regular time updates to keep everyone on task. When time is up, gather the group together and review all the bridges before agreeing a winner.

4. Paper Piers

Another simple activity that works well with groups of three.

Aim
To work cooperatively to construct a newspaper pier.

You will need
- Newspaper (broadsheets are best)
- Sticky tape
- A table for each group to work on

How to do it
Assign each group of three young people a table to work on, old newspapers and a roll of sticky tape.

The task for this activity is for each group to plan and build a paper pier from the edge of the tabletop as far as they can. Explain at the start that it is permissible to build struts to support the pier as it grows. In fact, it may be worth pointing out that the challenge is almost impossible if they don't. The pier can also be secured at one end to the table.

Allow between 15 to 20 minutes, dependent on how big your whole group is, for the young people to work on their constructions. Then call 'time' and review each design together. The longest pier wins the challenge.

The National Youth Agency

5. Cooperation Circle

This activity needs plenty of space and a large group to work well. If you have less than ten young people the task will be too easy and the cooperation element lost.

Aim

To create a group circle by working together.

You will need
• Nothing

How to do it

Clear a large area and ask the young people to stand in a circle holding hands, facing inwards. Place yourself in the middle so that everyone can see you. Explain that you are going to set the group a task that will need concentration and cooperation to work properly. Warn the group that if they don't work together they could all end up on the floor!

Ask the young people to turn to their right, making sure that they don't move out of the circle, and place their right hand onto the shoulder of the person in front. Now, instruct the young people to sit down carefully onto the lap of the person behind them, using their hand on their neighbour's shoulder to steady them. With a bit of practice, good balance and cooperation the whole group should be able to work together to achieve the task.

Once the young people have managed it, ask the group to slowly resume their standing position in the circle, making sure nobody falls. When the circle is once more complete give each other a round of applause to end the activity.

6. Card Sorting Game

The larger the team the harder this task is and the more the young people have to cooperate with each other to do it!

Aim
To work together to complete the sets of cards in a given order.

You will need
- Two packs of cards for each team, shuffled ready to be used as a set

How to do it
Divide the main group into equal sized teams of six or more. Hand each team a shuffled set and ask for a volunteer to deal them out amongst the team. Each team member should be left holding a random assortment of cards.

Now tell the teams that their task is to display the cards face up on the floor into suits as fast as they can – however, there are rules!

- The cards must be laid out in packs as well as suits
- Only one card can be laid at a time

First team to finish should all stand up and shout 'SORTED!'.

Finally, review the process with the young people. Was it easy to cooperate? Did leaders emerge?

7. Who's in the Bag?
This is a less active game ideal for mixed ability groups.

Aim
To use communication and listening skills.

You will need
- A set of 'Who's in the Bag?' Cards for each team
- A small bag for each team

How to do it
Divide the large group into equal sized smaller teams and hand each team a set of cards inside a bag. If you have young people who have difficulty with written activities make your own cards using photos from magazines.

Working as a team, the young people should take it in turns to take a card from the bag, making sure not to show anyone else. They then describe the person as clearly and quickly as they can without using any names. So for example, 'VICTORIA BECKHAM', 'used to be in a famous girl band, married to a famous footballer and has two sons'. If the young person is unsure who the person is, place the slip back into the bag and ask them to take another. The task for each group is to listen carefully and successfully guess the identity of as many of the people on the cards as possible.

Call 'time' after 20 to 30 minutes, depending on the size of your group, and ask the teams to count how many cards they have correctly identified – each card is worth a point. The team with the most points wins!

Who's in the Bag? Cards

VICTORIA BECKHAM	MICHAEL OWEN
GRAHAM NORTON	OZZY OSBOURNE
GARETH GATES	JENNIFER LOPEZ
TONY BLAIR	HOMER SIMPSON
WILLIAM SHAKESPEARE	BUFFY THE VAMPIRE SLAYER
COUNT DRACULA	SUPERMAN
FATHER CHRISTMAS	AUSTIN POWERS
MADONNA	CRAIG DAVID
ELVIS PRESLEY	ALI G
THE QUEEN	MINNIE MOUSE
BRITNEY SPEARS	WILL SMITH
MICHAEL JACKSON	POPEYE

8. Alphabet Game

This is a good activity for young people with physical disabilities as it can be done sitting down.

Aim
To tell an improvised team story using the alphabet.

You will need
• Nothing

How to do it

Seat the young people in a circle where they can see each other. If you know that the group has literacy difficulties make up cards with the letters of the alphabet clearly written on and hand these out before you start. Consider using picture cards as this is often easier for dyslexic young people.

Now explain that as a team the task is to work together to tell a story using the letters of the alphabet and in particular the names of the group members. For example, 'One day Anna woke up and decided...', 'to go to the beach'.

Encourage the young people to support each other as the story progresses and allow the 'PASS' option for anyone who gets stuck. Keep the story going until you get back to 'A' again and then close.

Trust Building Activities

9. Trust Game

This is a good team activity to build trust and empathy.

Aim

The aim of this is to allow members of the group to experience being the 'trusted' and the 'trusting'.

You will need
- A scarf to use as a blindfold

How to do it

Identify a safe space that provides a kind of 'obstacle course' for the young people to navigate. Show the team and ask them to nominate a volunteer to go first. Explain that the point of this activity is to encourage trust in each other and to take responsibility for their own actions and the safety of others. Tell them that if they feel really uncomfortable at any point they should say and the activity will stop.

Ask the volunteer to step forward and blindfold them. Make sure that they cannot see and ask them to describe how that feels. Lead the young person, with their eyes still covered, to the space you have identified for the session. Choose another member of the group to lead the volunteer. Explain that the role of the rest of the group is to support the young person who has the blindfold on.

Facilitate as the young people negotiate the course that you have chosen. Ask them to reflect on their feelings, particularly if the young person leading loses concentration or is careless in their directions. Then reverse the process.

Ask for feedback when everyone has had a turn. How did it feel to be dependent on someone? Was it better to be led or the leader? Did it make a difference if you could choose your partner? How did it feel if they gave you bad information?

10. Trust Game by the Sea
This is the same as the last activity, except you need to be by the sea!

Aim
To build trust and empathy within the team.

You will need
- To have checked the area of beach you intend to use and made sure that it is safe
- A scarf to use as a blindfold

How to do it
Explain that the idea of the exercise is to build trust between members of the group and for individuals to take responsibility for their own actions and the safety of others. One participant will wear a blindfold and another will lead them around the beach close to the sea, taking care that no one gets wet.

Ask a volunteer to step forward and blindfold them. Make sure that they cannot see and ask them to describe how that feels. Choose another member of the team to lead them.

As the young people negotiate the beach ask them to reflect on their feelings, particularly if the young person leading loses concentration or is careless in their directions. Then reverse the process.

Ask the group for feedback when everyone has had a turn. How did it feel to be dependent on someone? Was it better to be led or the leader? Did it make a difference if you could choose your partner? How did it feel if they let you get wet?

11. Silent Touch

The larger the team the harder this task is.

Aim

This activity builds trust and highlights the importance of non-verbal communication.

You will need

· Nothing

How to do it

Explain the aim of this game and agree ground rules around personal space and the need to stop if anyone feels uncomfortable at any point. Make sure that you stress that the young people should try and keep what they do, apart from the element of silence in the second part, the same. The idea is not for them to try and disguise their touch, but to utilise their senses in a different way. Ask for a volunteer to go first and invite them to stand facing a wall with their hands, palms down, touching it. They should stay looking at the wall throughout the whole process. Now, the rest of the group in turn walks up to the volunteer and places one hand on their shoulder, quietly saying their own name as they do it.

When everyone has done this they should do it again in a different order, but this time without saying anything. Relying only on the recognition of touch and their other senses the volunteer should try and guess who is touching them. Each member of the team should take a turn at facing the wall and guessing their teammates' identities.

Keep a tally of how many they guess correctly but do not discuss it as it may give clues to the young people who follow. After everyone has had a go announce the scores and review the process. How easy is it to identify people without seeing them? What senses were used? How did it feel?

12. Group Fall

You need to do a risk assessment for this activity. Make sure your instructions are clear and understood or you could end up with an accident.

Aim
To appreciate the importance of trust within a team.

You will need
• Nothing

How to do it
Ask the young people to form a circle, including yourself and your co-worker. This will need to be fairly close together with enough space to move quickly to successfully complete the task. Now ask for a volunteer. Be careful here that the first volunteer is not someone universally unpopular within the group or who is very nervous and unlikely to feel comfortable. Once you have a volunteer invite them to move to the middle of the circle and ask them to close their eyes.

Explain that the idea of the 'Group Fall' is to highlight the need for trust within the team. The young person in the middle will 'fall', still with their eyes closed, and as a group you are going to catch them.

Review the activity as you go along. How does it feel to have your eyes closed and place your trust in others? How does it feel to be responsible for the safety of someone else? What feels more comfortable? Continue the activity until everybody has experienced both roles.

Group Tasks

13. Brick Task

This competitive exercise works well with large groups of young people.

Aim
Teams work together to build a brick block to a prescribed pattern.

You will need
- Lego or building bricks – 12 each of six different colours
- Six large envelopes
- A marker pen

How to do it
To prepare, check out your own building skills and build a block with bricks of one colour, using a minimum of 12 bricks. Then get together enough bricks to make six more blocks of an identical size and shape, but in different colours.

Take the large envelopes and with a marker pen write the name of each colour block on the front.

Now, break up the blocks and muddle up the pieces into six piles – with the right number of bits to make the shape, but in mixed colours.

At the start of the session, divide the young people into six teams and ask them to set up team bases around the room. Hand each team a sealed envelope and explain that the task is to build a brick block in the colour written on the team envelope by negotiating and cooperating with members of the other five teams.

There are four rules:

1. Only one team member can leave the group at a time.

2. Only one negotiation can be happening within a team at any time.

3. No one can steal a piece from another group – cheating means disqualification!

4. No group can hold more than 12 pieces in their base at any time.

Allow 20 to 30 minutes to complete the task, asking each group to build their block and sit down in their base area as they finish.

Facilitate a feedback session. What happened? How easy was it to negotiate when you all had the same goal? Did a leader emerge from within the group? What would have happened if members had not cooperated? What would you do differently next time?

14. Stranded!

This is a discussion-based activity for groups of four to eight young people. The theme can be varied to suit the group.

Aim
To use collective knowledge and opinions to agree a group solution.

You will need
• A 'STRANDED!' list for each young person
• A pen each

How to do it
Invite the young people to sit in a circle and listen as you read out the following scenario;

'A light aircraft makes an emergency crash landing leaving a small group stranded in a dense tropical forest on the edge of a swamp. It is very hot and humid and starting to get dark.

All radio contact was lost about an hour ago, so no one at air traffic control can advise you or knows where the plane landed. You could be hundreds of kilometres from the nearest town and any rescue operation will not know where to start looking.

Suddenly someone shouts 'Quickly! The plane is about to burst into flames! Get out fast!'. You realise the group only has a few minutes to grab some essentials and leave.

Apart from what you are wearing, which does not include a coat, you have nothing with you except your mobile phone. It is possible that you could pick up a signal, but unlikely. What should the group take with them to try and survive until they are rescued?

Now hand the young people a 'STRANDED!' list and a pen each. Ask them to spend five minutes looking through it and ticking with their pen the articles that they think are the most important for survival. Stress now that there are no 'right' answers. This should stop the young people trying to guess what answer you want so they can concentrate on the process properly and come to their own decisions.

Then divide the large group into teams of between four to eight members and invite them to take their lists and use these as a basis for agreeing a team list. The rules for this are;

1. Only ten items can be taken from the plane.

2. All items must be agreed by the whole team.

3. Teams cannot take part of something or split goods.

4. Teams will need to nominate a speaker to share their decisions with the rest of the group towards the end of the exercise.

Allow the teams 30 minutes to discuss and agree their lists. During this time you can answer questions about the plane crash and the circumstances the survivors find themselves in, but you cannot offer any opinions!

Invite each team to present their list and explain their choices. How easy was it to agree the list? Did it help that you were in a group or was it easier to make your own decisions in the first part of the activity? What are the benefits of a teamwork approach?

'STRANDED' list

- One box of tea light candles (20)
- A compass
- An inflatable dinghy
- An oar
- One pack of cans of fizzy drink (24)
- A basic first aid kit (including scissors, plasters and antiseptic cream)
- A can of fly spray
- A box of chocolate bars (36)
- Three large boxes of matches
- A torch and a pack of batteries
- A mobile phone (half charged)
- A pad of paper and a pencil
- A bag of fresh oranges (20)
- A one gallon drum of fresh water
- A solar powered calculator
- A small shovel
- A fire axe
- A large tarpaulin sheet
- One crate of bottled beer (36)
- Two distress flares
- A pack of firelighters (12)
- Six fire blankets
- Two large cans of insect repellent
- One box of mini bags of peanuts (72)
- Three rolls of toilet paper
- A needle and thread
- One roll of large black rubbish bags (12)
- Two decks of cards
- 20m of rope
- 12 cushions
- Eight cans of baked beans
- A whistle
- A Swiss Army penknife

15. Machine Race
This activity is a simple version of Scrapheap Challenge or Robot Wars!

Aim
For each team to work together to design and construct a model to race.

You will need
- A good selection of old boxes (cereal, shoe, egg etc)
- Sticky tape
- Wooden kebab skewers
- Scissors
- Cardboard tubes
- Paper
- Pens
- PVA glue
- Cotton reels
- Rubber bands
- Bricks and a piece of plywood (or similar) to make the slope

How to do it
Ask the young people to work in small teams of three or four and give each team a good selection of modelling equipment from the list above. Explain that the challenge for each team is to design and build a machine using the materials given that they can enter into the Team Race later.

Stress that they should spend time planning their vehicle and that all members should agree each stage of development. Make paper and pens available for those who like to draw things first.

Allow an hour for the planning and construction process, during which time you can set up the 'ramps' for the race using the bricks and a large sheet of plywood or similar. This doesn't have to be too sophisticated so feel free to improvise!

Facilitate races of three machines at a time, encouraging the other young people to support the teams. Keep the challenges going until you have an overall team winner! Review the process with the young people, in particular how it felt to work together as a team.

16. Design a Game

For this to work well you need to be working with young people of similar ability and age.

Aim

For small teams to design a game that can be played by all the teams.

You will need

- Scissors
- String
- Dice
- Building bricks
- Newspaper
- Flipchart paper
- Magazines
- Glue
- Coloured markers
- Playing cards
- Props box

How to do it

Place all the equipment you have collected together in the middle of the room so that it is available for all the teams. Make sure you have a good selection of things to use so that the young people can be as creative as possible.

Divide the young people into teams of three or four and explain that their task is to design a game that can be played by the whole group in their teams. Set some ground rules, for example, that the game should take ten minutes to play and that all team members must a have a role. Each game must also come with a set of rules.

Encourage them to be as creative about their ideas as possible. If you want to link this with issue-based work then offer a theme for the games, for example, drug awareness.

Allow 45 minutes to an hour for the young people to design and try out their games and then ask them to lay it out, with the rules, in front of their team area.

Each team then takes it in turns to go to a game and play it. When all the games have been played review the process with the young people.

17. Backwards Story
This works well with small teams of young people and requires concentration!

Aim
To work together as a team to tell a story from the end to the beginning.

You will need
• A dice

How to do it
Form a large seated circle to include you and any co-worker. Start the exercise with the end of a story. This can be as creative as you like but should end with something familiar to give the young people the idea. For example, 'and so the spaceship returned to earth, the world was saved for another day and they all lived happily ever after!'.

The dice is then passed around the circle, giving everyone the opportunity to think of what may have already happened in the story, until someone throws a six. They then have to take up the story and tell the bit that came before the ending.

Encourage the young people to keep their story simple as it will become very hard to follow if it gets too complicated and remind them that everything will need to be told in the past tense as it will already have happened!

The task is complete when the story has been told all the way through back to the beginning.

18. Picture Quiz

This is an adaptation of the traditional memory game that is effective with small teams.

Aim

To set a challenge for another team that relies on memory and shared knowledge.

You will need
• A copy of the same picture for each team
• Paper
• Pens

How to do it

Divide the group into teams of three or four. You will need at least two teams to compete against each other. Hand each team a copy of the same picture. This should be complex with lots of images and things going on in it. Teams then have 15 minutes to look closely at the picture and set 20 questions to ask another team about what they can see. For example, 'What colour is the little girl on the bike's t-shirt?'. These can then be written on the paper. After 15 minutes collect in all the pictures and set them face down away from the teams. Invite teams to swap questions so that each team has a new challenge. They now have ten minutes to use their collective memories to answer the questions set and write the answers on the sheet!

Hand the pictures back out so that the teams can assess how well they have remembered what they saw. If you want this to be competitive points can be awarded for correct answers and added up at the end. Review the process, in particular looking at how the young people agreed on what they had seen. Was it just one person with a good memory? How were differences of opinion resolved? Were some people better at remembering or thinking of the questions than others? How did this help the team in the task?

19. Trading Game

Aim
To develop negotiating skills within teams.

You will need (for each team)
- Six different types of sweets (wrapped in different colours)
- A sheet with the different worth of each sweet
- An additional three sweets

How to do it
In preparation for the session decide what 'value' you are going to place on each of the sweets. As this is a trading game this is important! It doesn't really matter what currency you choose, eg Euros or points, what is important is that you write a sheet up so that the young people are clear about what you are using. Then write up a scoring system that is in addition to the straight trade values of the sweets. This is my suggestion but you can adapt it as you want.

1. 30 bonus points for a set of all one type of sweet.
2. 20 bonus points for three different types in a set.
3. 10 bonus points for two different types in a set.

Divide the main group into teams of three and hand each team their set of sweets to trade with. Explain the rules and hand each team a sheet with the values and scoring system on it. Point out that anyone who eats the sweets loses all their points and their team is disqualified!

Now set the teams the task of trading with each other in a bid to collect the set that has the highest value. The purpose is to encourage the young people to plan their negotiations and work together to devise a strategy. Allow 30 minutes (longer if you have a lot of teams) before announcing that trading has ceased. Ask the teams to count up their scores and write the total on their sheet.

The team with the highest score wins and is given the spare three sweets as a 'prize'. Review the process and then invite the teams to eat their assets!

Outdoor Ideas

20. Break the Code

This is great fun to do at night, but you should ask the young people to bring a torch with them and be prepared to do a risk assessment in advance.

Aim
For teams to compete and be the first to solve the puzzle.

You will need
- To research the area and devise a sheet of instructions/questions based on local landmarks and sites. Copy one for each group
- A risk assessment
- Two torches
- Pens
- Four boxes with a small chain and combination padlock holding it shut
- Four keys for the padlocks

How to do it
Plan your instructions before the session. These should be simple and based on the local area. All of the answers should lead to numerical solutions that in turn will be the combination that you set on the padlock. For example, 'Walk to the end of the road and turn left. When you get to the bus shelter look up. Write down the middle number of the first line of numbers …'.

Prepare a box for each group. Place tissue paper and glitter inside and secure the box with a chain and combination padlock. You could put sweets, shredded newspaper, or anything you want into the box. Divide the young people into four teams. Explain that each team is going to be given a 'gunge bomb' to hold. Tell them that the only way to diffuse it is to break the code on the combination padlock holding the box shut. You can be as dramatic as you like over this bit!

Give out the instruction sheet and explain that the teams are competing against each other to be the fastest to follow the clues and solve the puzzle. Identify a meeting place where the youth workers will stay holding the keys. This is where the groups should come to when they think that they have broken the code.

Send each of the four groups off five minutes apart, making sure that one of the workers circulates around the area to support the groups and see that there are no problems.

Once the first group returns to the meeting place, they are allowed one go at defusing the 'gunge bomb'. If they are successful check their time and register it. If not send them off again.

Once all the groups have returned and opened their boxes check the times. The group that completed the task in the fastest time 'wins'. Review the process with the group.

21. Sand Holes

This is another activity for youth workers based by a beach. You will need to check out local tide information and complete a risk assessment before you decide to go ahead.

Aim

For teams to work together to complete a task in the fastest time.

You will need

- To complete a risk assessment
- Lots of sand
- One large black plastic bin liner per team

How to do it

Divide the group into teams of up to six young people. Issue each team with a bin liner. Explain that the aim of the activity is to complete the task as quickly as possible.

They will need to work together effectively to do this.

Then explain the task. Each group needs to dig a large, deep hole with their hands. They can do this together or in turns. When the hole is large enough for the smallest member of the group to get in – stop!

That person then gets inside the hole, using the black plastic bag to keep them dry. The rest of the group then needs to fill in the hole – with the person still inside – making sure that no sand is left on the side.

The first group to complete the task wins! Evaluate the process. How easy was it to work together? How did you decide roles? Who made decisions?

22. Plate Spinning

This team game is great fun and can be adapted to make the challenge as hard or as simple as you like!

Aim

To pass the spinning plate around the team without dropping it.

You will need

- A plate spinning set for each team (comprises of a plastic plate and a plastic, pointed wand to spin it on)

How to do it

Give each team of six young people a plate spinning set and allow them to practice so that they can spin the plate on the wand in the air. This is not as easy as it seems and you should practice yourself first so that you can do it too! Encourage young people who can do it to support other members of their team and help them master the skill.

The task is for each member of the team to be able to spin the plate five times and then pass it to the next person. This should be repeated until the plate returns to the person who first held it. It is up to individual teams to decide how they are going to achieve this, although you may want to suggest working in a circle.

If this is too difficult set the activity up as a relay and invite each team member to pick up the plate and wand, spin it five times and then place back down ready for the next person. The first team to complete the task wins!

23. Raft Race

This activity requires teams to work on water so you will need to do a risk assessment and consider the need for a qualified outdoor education instructor before you decide to go ahead.

Aim

To build and race a raft that will float and carry the team within a designated course.

You will need

- A safe area of water – lake, river or swimming pool
- Four empty oil drums for each team
- Rope
- A penknife (or similar to cut lengths of rope)
- Wood that will float (long logs or pieces of packing crates)
- Two paddles per team
- A stopwatch
- A qualified lifeguard or instructor

How to do it

Before you start go through the safety procedures that you have put into place so that the young people are clear about the boundaries and what to do if they get in to trouble. Get parental/carers' consent to take part and check out the swimming ability within the group.

Divide the young people into teams. The numbers will depend on how much material you have available, as this will determine the size raft the group can build. Teams of five or six young people are ideal.

Give each group the oil drums, rope, wood and a penknife and tell them that their task is to build a raft that they think will float and hold all of them. Explain that everyone must contribute to the design and that it cannot be tried out on water until the second part of the activity.

Allow 45 minutes for the crafts to be built and then ask the teams to stop. Review the process so far briefly, asking the young people to consider the roles that they played within the team and how tasks were delegated.

Now hand out the paddles and explain that the second part of the exercise is for each team to race their raft from one place on the water to another. Stress that it doesn't matter if people get wet on the journey, but all members of the team must still be on the raft at the end. Make sure that everyone is clear about the race area and where the 'finish line' is! Then allow five minutes for the teams to discuss who will use the

paddles, who will sit where on the rafts and who, if anyone, will lead. Explain that this time to agree tactics should be used carefully as it is important!

Invite all teams and rafts to make their way to the 'start line' and then start the race. Use the stopwatch to time the race and encourage the winning teams to support the other groups as they make their way to the finish line. Celebrate the completion of the task and review the process.

24. Team Quests
This is good finale activity or one for summer evenings!

Aim
For teams to complete the set task as fast as possible.

You will need
Three sets of the following;
- A hula hoop
- Three juggling balls
- A football
- A yo-yo
- Aerobic step
- Coloured, plastic sticky tape
- A whistle
- Instructions for each activity
- A written set of the rules clearly displayed

How to do it
Before the young people arrive set up five activity areas. Each area should contain three sets of one activity, for example, the juggling balls and three copies of the instructions for the task. Mark out a boundary box for each 'Quest' and also a 'start line' at a distance from the first activity.

Split the main group into three teams of at least five young people (no more than seven). Try and balance the mix of gender and ability within the teams. Explain to the teams that this activity is a contest to see which team can complete all five 'Quests' in the fastest time. The rules are;

- When you blow the whistle the contest begins
- All 'Quests' must be completed by every member of the team

- No member of a team can move onto the next 'Quest' until the last member has finished their round
- No member of any team can use force to obtain equipment
- If any team member is caught cheating the whole team is instantly disqualified
- The first team to complete all five tasks and return to the start line and sit down in height order wins!

Make sure that everyone is clear about the rules and show the young people where you have displayed them.

Blow the whistle and stand back, supporting each of the teams as they move through the different activities. When the first team to complete returns to the start line and sits down, declare their team the winner. Encourage the winning team to support the rest of the group as they finish the course and close by celebrating the team victory and the achievements of the rest of the group.

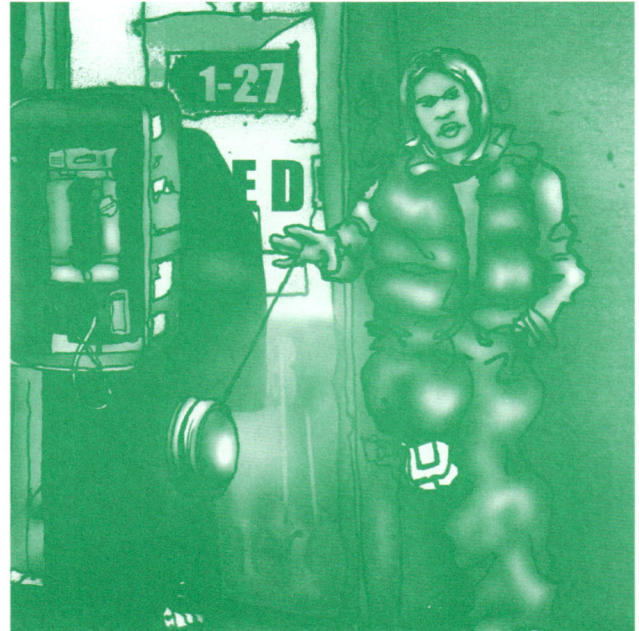

QUESTS

Juggling Balls
Each team member must juggle all three balls 20 times (three of which must be continuous).

Hula Hoop
Each team member must spin the hula hoop around their waist 15 times (three of which must be continuous).

Football
The team should stand in a line. The first person bounces the ball five times and then passes it over their head to the next person behind, who bounces it five times and passes it through their legs to the person behind them. Repeat the pattern to the end.

Yo-yos
Teams should stand in a circle and in turn throw the yo-yo ten times each (each member is allowed one fault before they have to begin again).

Aerobic Step
Each team member must complete 20 steps onto the block using alternate feet to step on and off.

25. Tennis Ball Challenge
This activity is ideal for use with larger teams. To make it a harder challenge keep adding tennis balls!

Aim
For teams to work together to complete the task in the fastest time.

You will need
- Two tennis balls per team
- A stopwatch

How to do it
Divide the larger group into two teams, with a maximum of ten young people in each team. If you have a really large group then allow for more teams. Ask each team to form a wide circle and hand one member a tennis ball. Explain that each team is in competition with the other groups. The team that completes the task in the quickest time is the winner. The task is to pass the tennis ball to every member of the team and back to the person originally holding it, without touching each other. This means that the ball must be thrown rather than passed. If the ball is dropped and hits the floor then the team has to start again. Facilitate a couple of rounds, using the stopwatch to time the teams. The team that wins each round is awarded a point.

Then throw in another tennis ball and explain that the young people now have to pass both balls around the team, with the same rules as before. You can extend the challenge to use three or four balls at a time if you want to make it harder!

Facilitate three more rounds at the increased level and then close. Add up the team points – the team with the most is the overall champion and can choose the next activity!

26. Number Challenge

This challenge is fun and should be facilitated at a fast pace. It is not suitable for young people who find reading tasks difficult.

Aim
Each team has to work together to devise the quickest way to meet the challenge.

You will need
• 60 paper plates for each team
• A black marker pen
• A stopwatch

How to do it
To prepare for the exercise mark up the paper plates with the numbers one to 60. Then carefully lay each team's set out in the same non-numerical order. Divide the young people into teams of six and show them the paper plates on the floor. Explain that the challenge is to touch the plates in numerical order as quickly as possible, competing against the other teams. If a plate is touched incorrectly then the challenge must begin again, and only one plate can be touched at a time. Additionally people are only allowed one go at a time. Encourage the young people to support each other as they work in their team.

After the first round share the quickest time and ask the young people to consider ways that they could speed up the challenge. The second time around set a time limit that is slightly shorter than the winning time from the last one. Continue with as many rounds as the young people are motivated for, decreasing the time limit each time. In between attempts facilitate a review of the process, considering how the teams are working together and what is helping them to achieve their goal. The overall winner is the team that completes the most rounds at the fastest speed.

27. Hula Relay

This works best with groups of twelve plus young people. To adapt it for smaller groups just use one hula hoop.

Aim
To devise a way of working together that enables the hula hoops to be passed around a circle.

You will need
- Two hula hoops
- A stopwatch

How to do it
The hula hoops used for this activity can be bought from most toyshops, but try and get the bendy ones rather than anything too rigid. Invite the young people to form a large circle and hold hands. Explain to them that this is a game of speed and skill and set two rules;

- When the game starts they cannot let go of each other's hands
- They must work together as a team

Unlock the joined hands of two young people, place the first hula hoop over their wrists, and then re-join their hands. On the opposite side of the circle repeat with two more young people. Once the hula hoops are in position remind the group that this is a task of speed and skill that they can only achieve by working cooperatively.

Now explain that when you say 'GO!' the clock starts and the two hula hoops should move around the circle as quickly as possible and back to their starting position. The first must travel clockwise around the circle and the second anti-clockwise. Remind the young people that their hands must stay locked together at all times!

The National Youth Agenc

Start the stopwatch and time the group as they wriggle through the hula hoops and work out how to move the hula hoop between them. Lead a group cheer as the hoops get back to their original place.

Now review the process and ask the young people to consider what they have learnt and how they could work together now to improve their speed.

Do it all again! Close by calling out the improved speed and cheering again.